MW00424515

How to Start a Shoe Design Business

ISBN-13: 978-1477696194

ISBN-10: 1477696199

HOW TO START A SHOE DESIGN BUSINESS

Essential Start-Up Tips to Boost Your Shoe Design Business Success

Becci Rolli

I dedicate this book to every person – be they woman (or man) whose lives have been touched by the joy, excitement and sheer fun of getting new shoes...

Contents

Shoe Design Business
An Introduction

If you have a natural love for fashion and a particular fascination with shoes, then you may want to consider getting into the shoe design business.

If you're naturally artistic, then this can be a very lucrative venture, and it isn't as difficult to get into as you may think.

It does involve work, but as long as you have a solid and creative product, then you'll definitely do well.

The challenge this career poses truly makes it a very dynamic field of design. Although it isn't really a requirement, a degree in fashion design will definitely provide you with a strong foundation that'll help you succeed in this business. More importantly, it pays to learn as much as you can about the field of shoe design so let's get started.

Unique field

Shoe design is often defined as a more focused approach to fashion designing, since professionals in this field concentrate on conceptualising, creating, and showcasing designs of no other clothing item but shoes.

There are even some shoe designers who decide to specialise even further by designing shoes only for a specific age bracket, gender, professional affiliation, or interest.

For example, there are businesses focused on designing shoes for children, for women, for nurses and nursing students, or for sports enthusiasts.

If you decide to become a shoe designer, then you have the choice of working for a corporate shoe retailer or footwear design company, or creating your own shoe design business.

Getting down to business

Establishing your own shoe design business, of course, involves more work than simply getting work as a shoe designer. Either way, you'll need to take some important steps so as to become a professional shoe designer.

Qualified

As mentioned earlier, a degree in shoe design isn't necessary, but if you do have either a 2-year or for 4-year degree in fine arts or fashion design, then you'll definitely be in a much better position to enter the shoe design business, which can be very competitive.

Knowledge

Generally you'll need to learn about fashion history, shoe engineering, industrial design, and fashion merchandising, among other things. And because shoe designers typically work independently, it'll definitely be of much benefit for you to get a basic education in business and marketing.

Skills

With or without the educational background discussed above, you can still succeed in the shoe design industry as long as you have the right set of skills.

Needless to say, you'll need a good grasp of the latest fashion trends and a deep understanding of the processes of industrial design and manufacturing.

Other than that, you'll also need artistic skills, including drawing skills, knowledge of fabrics and textures, and a good eye for colour.

And in the digital marketplace, it has also become increasingly important for designers to have skills with computer-aided design (CAD) programs.

A good grasp of biomechanics and podiatry is also very useful.

Choosing your route

While there are available staff positions for shoe designers in some shoe design companies and boutiques, these positions are generally scarce, which is why many shoe designers decide to build freelance careers or start their own shoe design business.

Furthermore, working for a boutique or shoe design company typically involves inconsistent pay levels that are usually based on your level of experience, target market, and reputation.

With the right skills and determination, though, it's entirely possible to earn a high income from and attain success with your own shoe design business the way Jimmy Choo and Manolo Blahnik did.

Education and training

While formal education may not really be necessary to succeed in a shoe design business, aspiring designers with an associate or bachelor's degree in fashion design usually hold an advantage and a competitive edge in the market. Fortunately, there are private design and art schools that offer focused design training programs you can enrol in.

You need to begin your formal shoe design training at the undergraduate level by obtaining an associate or bachelor's degree in fashion. There are a number of retailers and shoe design companies that hire professionals with associate degrees, but a majority prefers those who possess a bachelor's degree.

If you have a good combination of education (not necessarily fashion-focused) and experience, then you may no longer need further schooling. Take note that experience is vital in the field of shoe design and most of the popular designers these days started out as assistants and then worked their way up over the years.

Although associate and bachelor's degrees are the common avenues of training for shoe designers, there are also some certificate programs you can enrol in. These programs are typically focused on specific aspects of shoe design, such as athletic shoe design or women's shoes.

In most shoe design courses, students also get to develop skills in Adobe Photoshop and Illustrator, which are commonly used applications in the shoe design industry.

An Associate of Arts in Footwear Design or Applied Science in Footwear Design course may be completed in as little as a year, since most of these programs are geared towards fashion professionals seeking specialisation training. Students are generally taught about the history of shoe design, the different trends, the basic shoe styles, and shoe design tools.

In contrast, those who enrol in a Bachelor of Fine Arts in Fashion Design course need to complete core art studies on colour and form. Additionally, you'll also study sewing, sketching, pattern drafting, and general design before you can advance to shoe design specialisation.

With your specialisation courses, you'll learn about designing and creating specialty shoes like boots and theatre footwear. You're also likely to study closed-shoe design techniques and learn how to manipulate leather for creating shoes. Other than that, you also get to learn the fundamentals of marketing and merchandising.

Portfolio

While you're honing your skills in shoe design, you can also start building a portfolio of your designs. Students are generally given the chance to enjoy the benefits of fashion industry internships wherein they experience real-world shoe design training.

During these internships, you may observe and assist professional shoe designers, marketing representatives, and product developers. As a result, you learn about how to create, exhibit, and sell your shoes.

By the time you graduate from your shoe design course, you should already have built a good portfolio and may be able to find an entry-level job in a design or manufacturing firm. And once you've gained considerable experience in the field, you can start thinking about moving on to freelancing or starting your own shoe design business.

Career profile

As a shoe designer you will be responsible for creating shoes either for new or existing shoe lines and they typically take care of the entire process from conceptualisation to the actual creation of the shoes. With their knowledge of industry trends and design concepts, they sketch their designs either by hand or using CAD software. As soon as the design is completed, they use their knowledge of patterns and materials to create a prototype, which is then refined and used as model for creating samples to be presented in industry shows.

The level of involvement that a designer has in the entire shoe-making process will depend largely on their level of experience as well as the size of the company they work for.

It has been reported that the salary of shoe designers are quite inconsistent and depends largely on your experience and expertise.

You may have a greater chance of earning well if you start your own shoe design business as you will have ultimate control over how hard you work and what price you sell your designs / shoe products for.

Professional development

Having a degree in fashion design may not even be enough to ensure success in the shoe design business, since trends and preferences are constantly changing.

You may enhance your skills further by attending fashion shows to learn about the latest trends in style and color.

You can also do internet research, as there are a number of online fashion news articles and e-bulletins you can learn from. Fashion conferences and expos are also excellent venues for additional learning and may also give you the opportunity to network with other industry professionals and market your shoes.

Skills

A good eye for aesthetic detail is particularly important because you'll need to consider colour, lines, balance, and other specific design principles when you create your shoe designs. And even if you don't plan to physically create prototypes of your designs, you'll still need at least some basic knowledge in constructing shoes so you can communicate exactly what you want to see in the final product to whomever ends up manufacturing your shoe designs.

In connection to this, you need not only creative talent, but also a deep understanding of shoe engineering and good communication skills to be successful in a shoe design business.

Anatomy

Additionally, shoes are often created for specific purposes, such as football shoes, dancing shoes, and the like. For this reason, you'll need to acquire at least some basic knowledge on foot anatomy in order to come up with appropriate designs.

Marketing

Furthermore, you'll need the ability to push your designs into the market, which is why business and marketing skills are also very important in trying to achieve success in the shoe design business. In fact, more than half of the work you need to take care of each day will have to do with the business end of things rather than the design aspect.

Narrow it down

First of all, you'll need to decide what particular types of shoes you'll be designing and putting up for sale.

- Will you be offering all kinds of shoes or specialising in one or two specific shoe types?

- If you decide to specialise, will you be choosing your specialisation according to gender, age bracket, or interests?

- Will you be designing and selling shoes for women, for children, or for sports enthusiasts?

- If you decide to focus your efforts on sports shoes, you may even narrow down the specialisation further to offer only football or basketball shoes. Take note that athletic shoes are among the biggest-selling types of shoes all over the world, but you may have to battle it out with giant brands like Adidas and Nike if you choose to go this route.

Deciding on the particular type of shoe design business you'll be creating is mot critical and often overlooked. The type of shoes you decide to design will determine, to a large extent, the theme of your business and the kind of fabrics and materials you'll be using.

Subsequently, it'll also determine the amount of initial capital and financial backing you'll need for the business.

Customer is king

As you strive to break into the shoe design market, you'll need to offer consumers the kind of service that truly showcases your staff's courtesy and knowledge about your merchandise.

Take note as well that diversifying your product line is often more beneficial in the retail business, which is why you need to be able to offer a wide array of choices even if you're running a specialty boutique. For example, if you choose to sell women's party shoes, then be sure to offer designs in a variety of colours and sizes.

You should also make sure you have shoes for all types of women belonging to different age brackets. Your products should also come in a wide range of prices so you can cater to as many women as possible.

Buying patterns

Always remember that the shoe design business is extremely dynamic so you'll really need a basic understanding as to how you can convince consumers to buy your shoes. An excellent way to gain such understanding is to study the buying patterns of your target market.

Price

And as mentioned earlier, pricing is very important because it can be the primary reason why people decide to buy your products or choose the competition. The tendency of a person to buy something increases as the price goes down and people are also likely to buy more of your products the lower your prices are.

This doesn't mean, of course, that you should offer your products at prices that are too low because many people are also wary of products that are too cheap and they're likely to doubt the quality of your shoe range. You therefore need to learn the right balance where you set your prices.

Adapt

Remember as well that it's essential for you to adapt to your environment even as you focus on designing and selling specific types of shoes.

For example, if your shoe business caters primarily to women and is located near a dance studio, then it's a good idea to keep a sizeable stock of dancing shoes on hand. You'll have to study what the women in your surroundings want and then design your shoes according to their preferences.

Trends

Finally, you'll need to always keep up with the latest fashion trends, since this is really the main factor that dictates customers' choices. Among other things, you'll have to make sure the shoes you design can keep up with the latest New York or Paris fashion.

Other than fashion trends, you should also keep up with economic signs and strive to be insightful on market trends so you can adjust your shoe design business accordingly.

Business skills

Acquire the necessary business skills. Easy to say I know. But if you don't have a business degree, then you may want to consider enrolling in a fast-track or short course on business at the local community college.

It's also a good idea to attend business seminars and workshops to develop some business acumen. Take note that a large part of the venture will focus on the business rather than the design part, which is why it's as important to be a good businessman as it is to be a good designer when you start your own shoe design business.

Popular styles

Once you've decided exactly what type of shoes you'll be focusing the business on, you need to start familiarising the popular styles and brands in your chosen shoe market. To make sure your shoes sell, you may have to tailor them according to the latest trends. It may also be quite useful to study the history of popular brands and learn from their success story. Try to learn the ins and outs of the industry by keeping up with the latest news.

Storyboard

Make your own storyboard. A storyboard is basically a visual representation of your shoe designs, which encompass a single trend. This may be one of the currently popular trends, one of the trends of your favourite designer, or an original trend you hope to popularize. Take note that a storyboard doesn't have to consist of purely sketches you've made by yourself. It can include magazine clips, fabric swatches, your initial sketches, and your notes on each design.

Create your business plan

In order to convince potential investors that your idea for a shoe design business is sound, you'll have to develop a solid business plan covering at least the first five years of operations.

This plan should include an executive summary, your financial projections, and market research, among other things.

The market research portion should tackle important issues such as competition and trends. Your business plan should also discuss the different ways in which your prospective investor can invest. Your plan should include trends and competition analysis and financial study (estimated start-up expenses, profit projections, etc.), among other things.

Look book

Create a look book. Don't be confused between a look book and a storyboard. The storyboard is for your own use and serves as a guide for the creation of the shoes that you design. On the other hand, a look book serves as a sort of brochure or catalogue of your product offerings.

You may present it to prospective investors to give them an idea regarding the quality of your designs. And when your business finally opens, you can present the look book to potential customers as well to give them an idea of what you have to offer.

When you prepare your look book, you shouldn't be afraid to let your creative juices flow. After all, creativity is the key to good design. However, you should also strive to give your look book a professional appearance. A good way to learn how to do this is to check out samples of look books online.

Present to investors

Now you're ready to start making presentations to potential investors. It's a good idea to choose investors who focus primarily on new businesses.

Create a visual presentation of your shoe designs encompassing a specific trend.
You can choose to follow a popular trend or create your own. Your presentation may include sketches, fabric swatches, magazine clips, and notes. Sketches are especially important because they show your potential backers how artistically creative you can be.

Be sure to choose investors who are known to focus on new businesses so you'll stand a better chance of getting financial backing. This is your chance to make good use of your business plan and look book so make it worthwhile.

Get a manufacturer

Find a good manufacturer, negotiate a good deal with them, and then arrange to have samples of the shoes you designed made. Speak with a few different manufacturers before making your final choice.

Most shoes are manufactured in Italy, China, or Portugal. It's a good idea to contact two or more manufacturers and then go with the one that offers the best deal. Once you've got samples of your shoes made, you can make the final edits and finalise the designs before getting an entire shoe line manufactured.

You can also use the samples to start showing off your work and marketing your business to your target market.

Establish a solid business partnership with your manufacturer is vital so you can ask them to make quick samples in the future.

Trade shows

Find out which trade shows in your area get the highest traffic and then sign up for those that most appropriate for your shoe design business. Take note that you don't have to limit yourself to trade shows featuring shoes. If you're planning to sell women's shoes, for example, you could participate in wedding fairs where you can display your wedding shoes collection.

Familiarize the brands and styles in your chosen niche. Read up on shoe design and start-up businesses. Check out Footwear News and WSA Today for more know-how and to get industry secrets.

Get help

As you begin to turn your dream of running a shoe design business into reality, you shouldn't expect to do all of the work by yourself.

Chances are good that you don't possess all the qualities and skills needed to turn the business into a success. You may need to hire technical pattern makers, sales representatives, web designer or publicists.

And, of course, you'll need to have a solid relationship with your manufacturers. Be careful not to sign any deal with a manufacturer without thoroughly reviewing the agreement and never pay for the full cost of manufacturing upfront.

So now we have covered the overview let's get down to specifics.

Naming Your
Shoe Design Business

Choosing a company name can be the most fun part of starting a company. It can also be one of the most important.

After all, having the right shoe design business name can be a very effective advertising tool.

Among other things, it can give prospective customers a general idea of what your company does and what you have to offer.

In the same way, choosing the wrong name is likely to drive would-be customers away.

Here are a couple of things to remember when choosing a shoe design business name:

Keep it short and memorable

Needless to say, a short company name is much easier to remember than a lengthy one.

Choosing a short name doesn't just involve using less words, but also words with less syllables.

But, aside from being short, your shoe design business name also has to be catchy so as to promote better name recall.

You are your name

This means your company name should reflect the company's personality.

It should give people a general idea of what services you provide or what benefits they can get from patronizing your shoe design business.

You need to have an image which you want your shoe design business to project and the name you choose must fit that image.

More importantly, you have to choose a name your target customers can easily connect with.

Now, you know the basics of choosing a company name and you realize how important a name is to your business.

However, you shouldn't take the process of choosing a name too seriously.

While the company name does have to reflect its personality, it doesn't really have to define your company completely.

Take note that venturing into other related businesses is a normal part of any company's growth, so there is a real possibility that you may have to change your shoe design business name from time to time.

Again, the name of your shoe design business is important, but you shouldn't get hung up on the process of choosing it.

As long as you make sure that it's memorable, it tells people what your shoe design business is about, and you're proud of it, then you're good to go.

Drawing Up a Business Plan

Developing a new shoe design business naturally requires a good foundation, and building such a foundation begins with having a sound business plan. Remember that the business plan is an essential part of documenting a start-up business' financial goals, business objectives, and marketing plans.

Implementation of all your shoe design business ideas can only successfully begin once you've completed your business plan.

Choosing the Right Format

You probably already know that a business plan ranks among the most vital components of starting your shoe design business and ensuring its success.

But, how exactly do you make a good business plan?

Well, there are several variations and templates you can choose from. What's important is for you to choose the one that's best suited to the kind of enterprise you'll be running and to the purpose for which you're making the plan in the first place.

Here are some of the things you need to take into consideration:

1. Your Target Audience

There are two types of business plan.
a. There are business plans intended for an internal audience and these plans are usually part of your shoe design business growth strategy; they're also usually referred to as strategic plans.

b. There are also plans meant for external audiences and the purpose of these plans is usually to attract financing, suppliers, or talent for your shoe design business.

If the purpose of your business plan is primarily to get funding, then the document will typically be in condensed form, or a sort of summary of a more comprehensive business plan.

Such a version is generally known as a *funding proposal* or a *business opportunity document* and it's usually followed by the larger plan.

A business plan can indeed be a very useful document, so it's important to clearly define the audience for which it is intended.

2. What Goes Into the Plan?

Remember that a business plan needs to be comprehensive and that it's essentially created to put into writing what you envision for your shoe design business venture.

Your shoe design business plan should contain:

- An executive summary,
- The background and history of your company,
- A clear description of your shoe design business concept,
- Your marketing analysis and development plan,
- Your operations and production assessment,
- Your financial assessments and projections,
- Your human resources management assessment and plan,

- Your business implementation plan,
- An identification of resources,
- The proposed investor deal structures wherever appropriate,
- A survival strategy that describes potential risks and mitigation measures,
- Your shoe design business growth strategy,
- Your exit strategy,
- Appendices.

If that seems daunting, don't worry.

Some of the components of your business plan may be longer than others and some of them are optional, depending on your target audience, the format you choose to adopt, and the purpose of your plan.

What's important is for your intended reader to clearly grasp the value proposition, understand why your shoe design business is expected to succeed, and how that success will be achieved.

If you're pitching the plan to potential investors, (or most probably the bank) then they should quickly understand your proposed deal structure and the possible returns.

3. What Length To Make Your Plan

The average business plan typically consists of 20 pages, though there are some that contain a hundred pages or more. The length of your plan will depend largely on its purpose and your target audience.

If the primary purpose of your business plan is to attract investors, then you can expect it to contain more details and therefore be lengthier than a plan that's primarily for communicating your shoe design business growth strategy.

In the same way, the business plan for a venture with a relatively simple concept should be a lot more concise than one that's made for a highly complicated enterprise.

4. Should You Use a Template or Pay a Consultant?

Many people are also confused as to whether they should hire a consultant to help them write their business plan or simply use a template for guidance. Well, it can be quite tempting to use a template or get someone else to make the plan for you. However, it's still best if you write the plan yourself even if you do decide to get some guidance from a consultant.

After all, who knows your business better than you?

A solid business plan is perhaps the easiest way for you to communicate your shoe design business ideas to your target audience as well as to help you prevent problems and identify business growth strategies.

It can also be your most valuable tool when you're in search of funding for your shoe design business.

Remember, though, that instead of treating it as a blueprint or a strict manual which you should implement to the letter, the plan should be seen as more of a guide in operating your shoe design business.

TIP: Even if you don't have an immediate audience for your plan, the document and even the process itself will definitely prove to be of value to your business in the long run.

Preparing a solid business plan for all the right reasons can indeed increase your chances of attaining success in your shoe design business.

How to Write the Executive Summary

The executive summary generally serves as the introduction to your formal and comprehensive business plan.

You could even say that this is Part 1 of your business plan.

It contains a summary of your shoe design business proposition, present business status, financial projections, and the key elements for success.

Although it's often tempting to just rush through this component of your business plan, always remember that an executive summary is likely to be the very first thing your target investors or banking officials will read in the document.

It basically tells the reader the status of the company currently, and where it's expected to go. Many people aren't likely to read the remainder of the plan if the executive summary doesn't catch their interest, so it's really very important to do this right.

The importance of the executive summary lies in the fact that it tells your reader exactly why you believe your shoe design business will be a success.

Brevity is the key to a solid executive summary, which generally ranges from half a page to a maximum of two pages. Writing anything longer puts you at risk of losing the reader's attention and appearing unfocused. If you can keep the summary under one page without sacrificing quality, then do so.

Note: Although it serves as the introduction, it's best to write the executive summary after you've completed your business plan. After all, it is basically a shorter version of your plan.
To keep the summary consistent
 with the plan itself, it should have the following components:

1. Your Mission Statement

Your business plan's executive summary is the best place for you to express your mission statement. Make sure that statement is concise and explains in as few words as possible the existence of your shoe design business, its goals, and how you plan to achieve those goals.

In short, it should explain your shoe design business thrust to the reader.

Remember to keep your mission statement focused and direct, leaving no room for confusion as regards what your shoe design business venture is all about.

2. What's Your Business Concept?

In describing your shoe design business concept, you'll need to offer some details about the kind of shoe design business you'll be running, who your target customers are, and what your competitive advantages are.

You may point out that you're filling a void you've identified in the market, offering better prices for comparable services in the industry, or offering a better service than what's currently available.

3. A Little Background

You may also want to give your reader an idea of when your venture began, who the founders are and what functions they perform, how many employees you have (or plan to hire), and where the shoe design business is located and if there are any subsidiaries or branches. A description of your offices and facilities as well as the services your offer would also be a good idea.

4. Your Shoe Design Business Status and Financial Outlook

You'll also need to give a short description of the current status of your shoe design business. Explain if your business is still in the conceptualization stage, if you've already started setting it up, or if it's already fully operational and you're simply planning to expand.

You should also mention your expected costs and your financial projections for both the short term and the long term.

This will give potential investors an idea of how much capital you need and if your business venture matches the kind of opportunity they're currently looking for. If you already have existing investors, then you'd do well to provide some information on them as well.

5. Key Factors for Success

The reader of your business plan will also appreciate getting a preview of the key factors for shoe design business success. These factors depend on your situation, of course, but it generally includes technology patents, strategic partnerships, market factors and economic trends.

If your shoe design business is already fully operational and you've had some successful projects worth noting (you may have been the first to offer a certain service in the industry), then you should include that as well.

Finally...

All in all, your business plan's executive summary should provide its reader with a quick but insightful glimpse into the plan itself.

It's advisable to highlight everything except the mission statement in bulleted lists. Include all of the important points without revealing too much, since each section is discussed in detail within the plan itself, anyway.

More importantly, make sure the summary sells the proposal on its own as much as possible, just in case reader doesn't read your plan. It does happen!

Note: It's also a good idea to draw up a table of contents right after the executive summary so the reader will know where he can find each section in the plan itself. If you're still in the process of setting up your shoe design business, then you likely won't have much to write as regards to some of the areas listed above. In that case, focus on your own experience and expertise in the field, and the circumstances that led to your shoe design business concept.

Tell your target readers how you plan to set your shoe design business apart from the competition and convince them that there's indeed a need for your business within your target niche or industry.

Company History

After the executive summary, your business plan should contain a section covering your business background or company history. The length of this portion and how it's told will depend largely on how far along your shoe design business is in terms of operations and development.

Naturally, the business history of a venture that's just starting is totally different from one that's been operating for some time. It should be about one page long, though it's understandable for a start-up company's history to cover less than an entire page.

What to Include

In this section, you should be able to illustrate how the various elements of your shoe design business venture fit together and form one successful enterprise.

You should also include some background information on the nature of the shoe design business itself and identify the factors that are expected to facilitate its success.

Furthermore, don't forget to mention the specific market needs you're planning to satisfy and the ways and methods in which you expect to satisfy these needs. If possible, you should also identify the specific individuals or groups of people whom you believe have those needs.

An example of a specific market could be:

Mena and women aged 18 to 30 with an income of $50,000 within 50 miles of your location.

How It All Started

Among the things you should include in the company history portion of your business plan is the origin of your shoe design business concept.

This explains how you first came upon the idea for your shoe design business and why you decided to pursue that idea. You should also indicate the progress you've made so far as regards operating and growing your business venture. If you're still in the process of starting your business, then say so.

NOTE: It's also a good idea to mention the problems you've encountered along the way and how you handled each of them. Potential investors and business partners will surely appreciate knowing that they're dealing with someone who's not afraid to deal with challenges from time to time.

Projected Short-Term Growth

You would also do well to include your short-term business growth plans in this section, so the reader will know that you've thought about your venture carefully and that you have concrete plans for its growth. If you're just starting a new shoe design business, then you may want to include a bit of personal history along with your background. Among the things you can include are your educational history, technical skills, areas of expertise, relevant professional club memberships, and other shoe design businesses you may have started or companies you worked for. You may even want to share your areas of inexperience or weaknesses and how you intend to compensate for these areas. Your target investors would definitely appreciate knowing that you're aware of the things you need to improve on and are making concrete efforts at improving them.

Finally...

In summary, the company history section of your business plan should provide an interested reader with a much better idea of how your shoe design business came to be and who you are as a businessperson. Again, the key is to keep this section concise and avoiding unwanted information.

Organization and Management

This section of your plan includes the following:
- Your company's organizational structure

- The profiles of your management team

- Details about company ownership

- The board of director's qualifications

It's important for you to answer the question of who does what when you prepare this section.

Explain what each person's background and qualifications are. Tell your reader exactly why you've brought or are bringing these people into your organization and management team.

What exactly are they responsible and accountable for?

NOTE: You may think this section of the plan is unnecessary if you're setting up a small venture with less than five people on your team, but anybody reading your business plan needs to know who's in charge.

Therefore, you should still provide a description of every department or division, along with their functions, regardless of the size of your company.

If there's an advisory board for your business, then you should also identify who's on it and how you plan to keep each member on the board.

- What salary and benefits do you plan to provide for members of your team?

- Will you be offering incentives? If so, what are they?

- How do you plan to handle promotions?

In this section of your business plan, you need to reassure your audience that the people on your team aren't going to be just names on your company letterhead.

What's Your Structure?

One very simple yet effective way of presenting your organizational structure is by creating an organizational chart and then providing a narrative description of the chart. By doing this, you don't leave anything to chance, you're making sure the functions and responsibilities of each team member has been carefully thought out, and you've ensured that someone's in charge of each and every function in your shoe design business. Therefore, no function is taken for granted and there'll be no overlapping of responsibilities. Remember that this kind of assurance is very important to your reader, especially if that reader is a potential investor.

Management Profiles

Ask any business expert and he'll probably tell you that among the most significant success factors in any business is the track record and ability of the management team. This is why it's important for you to provide your reader with a background of the key members of the management team. Specifically, you'd do well to provide resumes that indicate the name, position and the corresponding functions, primary responsibilities and level of authority, educational background, skills and experience, number of years on your team (unless it's a start-up company), compensation level and basis, previous employment and track record, industry recognitions received, and community involvement.

TIP: When you indicate the track record of your team, be sure to quantify their achievements.

For example, instead of saying:

"Extensive experience in managing a sales department"

you could say:

"Successfully managed a sales department of ten people for 15 years."

It's also a good idea to highlight how the key members of the management team complement your own experience and expertise.

If you're starting a new shoe design business, then show your reader how the unique experiences of each member of your team can contribute to your business venture's overall success.

Company Ownership

Aside from the organizational structure, this section of the plan should also describe the legal structure and provide important ownership information regarding your shoe design business.

- Has the business been incorporated? If so, then is it an S or a C corporation?

- Is your business a partnership?

- If so, then is it a limited or general partnership?

- Or are you the sole proprietor of your shoe design business?

The most important pieces of information you should include in this section are the owner/s' names, ownership percentage, form of ownership, degree of involvement of each owner within the business, common stock, and outstanding equity equivalents.

Board Qualifications

Take note that there's a huge advantage to setting up an unpaid board of advisors for your company, as it can provide you with the kind of expertise the company is otherwise unable to afford.

Simply by enlisting the help of some successful businessmen who are popular in the industry and including them in your advisory board, you'll definitely go far in enhancing the credibility of your company and encouraging a perception of expertise.

If the company has a board of directors, then you need to provide the names of the board members, their respective positions in the BOD, their background, the extent of their involvement with the shoe design business, and their expected contribution to its success.

Market Analysis

You may be a hundred percent confident about the quality of the service your shoe design business has to offer, but unless you're able to connect with your target customers, quality won't do you much good.
You'll have to get your service into your customers' hands, so to speak, to get the necessary sales.

And that's why you need market analysis.

This section of your business plan should be used to illustrate your knowledge of the industry. You may also use it to present highlights and conclusions from the marketing research data you've collected.

For your analysis to be reliable, you need to study the three Cs of marketing:

1. Company

2. Customer

3. Competition

Of course, it's understandable that you should be aware of your company's strengths and weaknesses, but you should also know the same things about your competitors so you'll get a better idea of how to deal with them.

More importantly, you need to know who your customers are and what their needs and wants really are.

When you prepare the company analysis component of this section, you'll need to describe the primary industry to which your business belongs, the industry's current size and historic growth rate, the industry's characteristics and trends, and the industry's major customer groups.

All these will put into perspective the description you'll provide of the company you've established or are planning to establish.

Who Are Your Target Customers?

In choosing and defining your target customers, make sure that you narrow it down to a size that you're sure you can manage.

Many business owners make the mistake of trying to provide everything to everybody at once. Slow and sure is often a better philosophy where your business is concerned.

This section of your plan should include information that identifies the unique characteristics of your target customers including:

- Their needs

- The extent to which these needs are being met

- Demographics.

It's also a good idea to identify your target market's geographic location, who among them makes the major decisions, and any market trends that may affect your business.

The size of your target market should also be indicated in this section, along with your expected market share gains and the reason for these expected gains.

You should also indicate your pricing schedule as well as your gross margin targets and whatever discount structures you may be planning.

You'd also do well to identify what resources you plan to use to get information as regards your target market, the media you'll be using to reach the market, your target market's purchasing cycle, and the socio-economic trends likely to affect your target market.
If all this sounds complicated don't worry, just break down each section and do it one at a time.

Your Competition

Of all the Cs you need to study, your competition may be the toughest, especially if you're new to the industry. The first thing you need to do is study your direct competitors.

If you're planning to operate a shoe design business in your district, then you're likely to get direct competition from the likes of the larger multi-national shoe design businesses. So it pays to examine all the possible options on how you can set your shoe design business apart.

It's important for you to identify your direct competitors according to product or service line and market segment.

You should then assess their weaknesses and strengths, determine the level of importance of your own target market to your competitors, and identify the barriers that may pose a challenge as you enter your target niche.
This may include high investment costs, changing technology, existing patents or trademarks, customer resistance, and a difficulty in finding quality personnel.

You'd also do well to determine the market share of each key competitor and then provide an estimate of the time it'll take for new competitors to enter the niche.

Aside from looking for ways to set yourself apart from the competition, you'll also want to see how your business fits into the marketplace itself.

In doing so, you'll have to consider the strengths and weaknesses of your competitors, the possibility of competitors leaving the marketplace and new ones entering it, the services your competitors are relying on for a majority of their revenue, and effective ways of overcoming possible threats from substitute services.

Developing Your Marketing Strategy

Once all three Cs have been addressed, you should be ready to start developing your marketing program. This basically involves an analysis of what's known as the "four Ps."

They are:

1. Product,

2. Place,

3. Price,

4. Promotion.

Product, of course, refers to what you plan to sell (in this case your shoe design service)

Place refers to where you plan to sell it (office, online, or both).

Price refers to the amount you'll charge for each service you'll be offering.

And Promotion refers to the incentives and other promotional strategies you plan to use in order to get your target market to try your services.

To put it simply, a marketing strategy is your way of drawing in customers, which is indeed very important since customers are essentially the lifeblood of any business venture.

There isn't a single way of approaching a marketing strategy. What's important is for your strategy to be uniquely applicable to your shoe design business and part of a continuing evaluation process that aims to facilitate business growth and success.

In conducting a "four Ps" analysis, you'll likely conduct some market tests and you'd do well to include the results of these tests in this section of your business plan. All other details of the tests may be attached as an appendix.

The information you provide in this section may include the number of customers who participated in the tests, demonstrations or any information provided to the participating customers, the degree of importance of satisfying the needs of your target market, and the percentage of participants who expressed desire to take advantage of your products and/or services.

After creating your marketing strategy, you'll also need to draw up a sales strategy, which outlines the methods you'll be using to actually sell the services you plan to offer.

There are two very important elements of a good sales strategy.

- The first is your sales force strategy, which determines if you'll be employing internal sales personnel or independent representatives. You should also identify the number of people you plan to recruit for your company's sales force as well as the recruitment and training strategies you'll be using. You'd also do well to present the compensation packages you've lined up for your sales personnel.

- The second element of a sales strategy is a description of the sales activities you've lined up for the company. A sales strategy is made more manageable when broken down into activities. For example, you could start with identifying prospective customers and then prioritizing your prospects according to those who have the highest potential of buying your products.

From this outline of activities, you can easily determine the number of prospects you may have to get to make a sale and the average amount you'll likely earn from each sale.

You'll also need to draw up a solid market development plan in order to make your market analysis work to your advantage.

While the information in your development plan is likely to come into play only when your company has been established and operational for at least a few years, potential investors will surely appreciate the fact that you've already envisioned your company's growth and evolution.

Among other things, your development plan should provide answers to the following questions:

➢ Is the market for the services you offer currently growing?

➢ Are you planning to offer line extensions or new services within your first few years of operations?

➢ Does the market development plan you've crafted offer ways of increasing the overall demand for your services within the industry?

➢ Are there alternative ways of making your company more competitive?

Remember that the market analysis is a vital part of your business plan and it's likely to take up a large part of the plan itself.

This is why it's necessary to conduct a thorough research on the competition and on the market you're planning to enter.

Finally…

You may have the best service in the market, but without an organized and well-crafted market analysis and development plan, you still won't be able to guarantee success. You market analysis helps you identify a clear roadmap of how to bring your services to your target customers.

Financial Projections

Making financial projections for a start-up shoe design business can be described as both science and art.

Investors may want to see you spell out financial forecasts in cold, hard numbers, but it's not really that easy to predict the financial performance of your shoe design business several years from now, especially if you're still in the process of raising capital.

Simply put, this is the part where you formally request funding from potential investors and you do that by illustrating how much funding you need for start-up as well as within the first five years of operations.

If you already have an existing business and are looking towards expansion, then you may reflect the funding requirements for the expansion itself.

Potential investors are also sure to appreciate some historical data as regards the financial performance of your company, particularly within the last three years or so, depending on how long you've been in business. If you have any collateral that can possibly be used to secure a loan, then that's worth noting as well.

Difficulty aside, financial projections are requirements for a solid business plan and you'll really have to deal with them if you truly want to catch your prospective investors' attention. Regardless of whether your business is a start-up or a growing venture, you'll still need to provide historical and/or projected financial data.

Here are a few useful tips:

1. **Don't let spreadsheets intimidate you**

All financial projections necessarily start with spreadsheet software, with Microsoft Excel being the most commonly used; chances are great you already have the software on your computer.

Other than this, there are also some special software packages that can help you with financial projections. These packages often provide flexibility, which allows you to weigh alternate scenarios or change assumptions quickly whenever necessary.

2. **Create short-term projections as well as medium-term projections**

Specifically, your prospective investors should see financial projections for the first year of operations, broken down into monthly projections.

You should also provide a three-year financial projection that's broken down into yearly projections and a five-year financial projection.

TIP: It's advisable, however, to keep your five-year projection separate from your business plan, but readily available in case a potential investor asks to see it.

When you project business growth, be sure to consider the current state of your market, trends in labour and costs, and the possibility of needing additional funding for future expansion.

3. Make sure start-up fees are accounted for

Never forget to include fees for permits, licenses, and equipment in your short-term projections.

You should also keep the difference between variable and fixed costs in mind when making your projections and differentiate between the two wherever necessary. Variable costs are usually placed under the "costs for goods sold" category.

4. Go beyond your income statement

While your income statement is the basic measuring tool by which projected expenses and revenue can be conveyed, a solid financial projection will go beyond that to include projected balance sheets that show a breakdown of your assets, liabilities, and equity, among other things.

You'd also do well to include cash flow projections that reveal cash movement through the company within a given period.

Estimates of the amount you plan on borrowing as well as expected interest payments on those loans should also be included.

Furthermore, you should make sure your financial projections are all in accordance to the GAAP.
TIP: If you're new to financial reporting or don't understand the last paragraph, then you may want to consider hiring an accountant to review your projections.

5. **Offer two scenarios only**

Although you need to go beyond the simple income statement, remember that where financial projections are concerned, potential investors really want to see only two scenarios: The best- and worst-case scenarios. Anything more than those two are superfluous and may just cause unnecessary confusion, so skip it.

Finally...

To sum up, this section should tell potential investors how much money you need now and in the near future, your preferred type of funding and terms, and how you intend to use the funds.

NOTE: Take note that the intended use of the funds is a vital piece of information for potential investors and would-be creditors, which is why you need to explain it in this section.

It's also important to include all pertinent business-related information that can possibly affect the future financial situation of your company. A trend analysis for your financial statements is also very helpful, especially if you present it with graphs, as this is easier to see.

TIP: Above all, you should strive to make reasonable and clear assumptions.

As previously mentioned, financial forecasting is both a science and an art. You'll need to make several assumptions, but you'll also have to be realistic when making those assumptions. Going overboard will likely raise red flags for potential investors, so always make sure your projections are backed up by solid research.

Calculating Your Start-up Costs

What are start-up costs?

These are the expenses you have to deal with before your new shoe design business can actually begin operations and earn revenue.

The concept of start-up costs is very important in tax law because these costs are not considered as deductible expenses, unlike most of the other business costs. You will, instead, need to amortize these costs over the course of a few months or years.

This means you'll only be able to deduct part of the start-up costs each year.

And you can only determine and take full deduction on your other expenses after you have determined start-up costs.

The first step

The first step in calculating the start-up costs of your business is to gather all of the expense receipts from business-related transactions.

Next, determine the exact date when your shoe design business opened and then separate the receipts into two piles: one pile for the expenses from before your business opened and another pile for expenses incurred after the opening day.

The next step is to remove all of the receipts for items such as research costs, taxes, and deductible interest from the pile receipts before opening day.
These costs can immediately be deducted.

Finally, add together all the remaining receipts belonging to your "before opening date" pile. The sum is your total start-up costs, which have to be amortized.

Amortization is usually set over a period of 18 months, and expenses like hiring and training costs, pre-opening advertising, and travel expenses to meet potential suppliers are usually included in the amortized start-up costs.

How to Obtain
Small Business Grants

When starting a business there can be some huge barriers standing in your way, among the biggest of which are start-up costs and other business-related expenses.

You may be planning to take out a loan for the purpose of starting your shoe design business.

Why don't you consider applying for grants from the government or from private organizations instead?

There are several reasons why grants are better than a loan, the most obvious of which is the fact that grants don't need to be repaid.

How exactly can you obtain a business grant and turn your simple idea into a thriving shoe design business? Read on to find out.

The Catalog of Federal Domestic Assistance is a good place for you to search for a specific grant you can apply for because it contains a list of all grants available for small shoe design businesses.

The catalog also indicates what type of business qualifies for a particular grant, so you can immediately determine which grants your shoe design business is likely to qualify for.

Another option is for you to visit the Small Business Administration's website, which promotes federal grant programs that offer almost $2 billion to small businesses, particularly those focusing on providing technological solutions to existing business issues.

Once you have identified the grant programs you will be applying for, you should start preparing a business plan.

Take note that grant organizations base their approval or rejection of your application on the contents of your shoe design business plan.

- Your plan should therefore include a statement of purpose that is clearly written and effectively defines the goals of your company.

- A good shoe design business description, an outline of your short-term and long-term goals, a discussion on planned marketing strategies, and a projected financial analysis should also be part of your plan.

The financial section of your plan is very important because organizations usually measure the worth of a candidate based on how you plan to use the grant money.

You should therefore make sure that your financial analysis and hypothetical budget are both conservative and realistic.

When your shoe design business plan is complete, it's time to create your actual grant proposal.
If you have previous experience in creating such a proposal, then you can save some money by writing the proposal yourself.

However, if you've never written a grant proposal before, then it would be wise to hire the services of a professional writer.

Make sure your proposal includes schematics, reports, and some basic information on planned projects that are likely to be influenced by the grant funds.

Furthermore, grant reviewers are likely to appreciate such attention to detail, which may be seen as a strong commitment to your product.

In this case, the reviewers will be more likely to approve your applying for grant funds.

Complete your grant application by including an updated list of contacts.

This list should start with the contact details of the top-level employees.

It should also include the contact details of individuals who can provide important details on the supplementary materials included in your application.

Make sure that all pertinent information on your shoe design business and requested files by the grant organization are included in your application.
If your application lacks any of these files, then the grant is likely to be denied or the processing could be very slow. Submit your application only when you're sure that it's complete.

It's also a good idea to have your grant application reviewed by family, friends, and colleagues so grammatical errors can be cleared up and anything you may have overlooked can be pointed out to you. And as a final review process, you should schedule a reading session together with your staff, so you can correct any identified problems.

Above all, you should be patient.

Take note that the process of getting approved for grants may take longer to complete than the process of getting approved for loans.

This is because grant applications are reviewed a number of times and most grant organizations have to go through thousands of applications at a time.

Getting Insurance for Your Shoe Design Business

So, you have an idea for a good shoe design business venture; you even have the name for your new shoe design business already.

And you've also proceeded to create a business plan and a proposal for a grant application.

What else do you need to do prior to actually operating your shoe design business?

You will need good insurance.

This is actually one of the most important steps you need to take when starting a shoe design business. The good news is that there are lots of great places where you can get good advice on the different types of insurance that you may need for your new shoe design business.

An insurance agent is probably the best person for you to approach if you're looking for advice on getting insurance for your shoe design business.

More specifically, you should hire the services of an agent for an insurance company that specializes on shoe design business insurance rather than a general insurance company.

You have to understand that you'll be dealing with a totally different set of risks and challenges with a business than you would with a car or with your home. Getting insurance from a company that specializes in shoe design business insurance assures you that the agent you're dealing with really knows what he's talking about.

You can expect the insurance agent to lay out several different insurance options for you.

These options can range from liability insurance for your shoe design business to auto insurance. You may also be offered property insurance as well as loss of business coverage, which protects your interests in case a fire breaks out and you end up without a business to run for a month or so.

It's important for you to ask questions and make sure you understand what each type of insurance covers you for so you can be sure to make an informed decision as to which types of insurance you're going to get. More often than not, you'll be presented with more insurance options than you can afford.

There's also a possibility that the insurance agent you're consulting will present you with more insurance options than your business actually needs.

This makes it even more important for you to understand what each type of insurance covers. Furthermore, the start of a business is usually a time when you will have to take a few risks by taking out less insurance than your shoe design business needs.

You'll have to decide how much you can afford to spend for insurance and which type of insurance is the most needed by your shoe design business.

Once you've determined this, you can leave the other types of insurance for later.

Most shoe design businesses start only with loss of business coverage, others with liability insurance.

The point is to get only the most important insurance coverage that you can afford for starters. As your company grows, it will become more important for you to protect your shoe design business' assets.

And the good news is that you may able to afford it at that time.

Aside from the insurance that you have previously identified as a need for your shoe design business, there may also be other types of insurance that your customers expect you to have.

You can work on getting these additional insurance types when the right time comes.

How to Trademark Your Business Name and Logo

If you have just put up a new shoe design business, you should be careful not to stop at choosing a name and logo for it.

You should also make sure that the name and logo you chose is adequately protected.

This is especially important if one of your business goals is to create an instantly recognizable brand. The best way to protect your business name and logo is to have it trademarked.

Take note that a trademark is also used to protect symbols, drawings, and any other character associated with your shoe design business, much like a patent protects inventions.

The whole process of getting your business name and logo trademarked is a relatively simple one. However, it often takes several months for your trademark registration to really become official.

Following is a quick guide on how you can protect your business name and logo by getting it trademarked.

1. Choose the name and design the logo for your new shoe design business.

    You have to make sure, of course, that the name and logo you choose are not yet being used by any other company.
    More importantly, you need to ensure that such name and logo have not already been trademarked by someone else.

You can check the database of the official trademark office to make sure you won't run into any legal problems with your chosen name and logo.

2. Once you have established that your chosen shoe design business name and logo are not yet trademarked, request for and fill-out the necessary paperwork.

   Once the paperwork has been filled out and submitted to the Patent and Trademark Office, the processing of your application for registration will officially begin.

3. Allow five months for the processing to be completed.

   If five months have passed and you still have not received any notification of your trademark having been filed, you may check on its status. Take note, though, that it usually takes between five and seven months for a trademark registration process to be completed.

4. Once you receive notification of your trademark having been filed, obtain a copy of it from the trademark office.

   Take note that you will be asked for your registration number when you make the request for a copy of your trademark certificate.

5. Between the fifth and sixth year of your trademark registration, make sure that an

"Affidavit of Use" is filed, so as to prevent other companies from using your trademarked name and logo.

You should remember to file two other affidavits as well before every 10-year period of owning the trademark has passed.

Writing an
LLC Operating Agreement

Limited Liability Corporation, or LLC, is the ideal set-up for start-up companies and small businesses because it requires the business owner to take on only limited liability for the company.

And the good news is that creating an LLC is fairly simple and inexpensive. Take note that the operations of an LLC are governed by the LLC operating agreement.

You'll therefore need to learn how to write your LLC operating agreement.

Here is a step-by-step guide:

1. Gather basic information such as the company name and location as well as the names and physical addresses of the members of your company. You should also note your agent's name.

2. Gather all financial information.

   This includes each member's initial contribution to the company and how much each of them will own in terms of percentage of company interest. You can choose to have either a single-member or multi-member LLC.

   For example, you could choose to initially make a contribution of $100 and own a hundred percent of the company.

   What's important is for all company members to be included in your LLC operating agreement.

3. Choose and download a sample agreement.

   Of course, you can choose to write your own agreement from scratch, but working from a sample would definitely make the process much easier for you.

   While operating agreements aren't really that complex, the language used can be very governmental, and basing your agreement on a sample will help ensure that the language is interpreted correctly.

4. Determine if you need the services of a registered agent.

   Take note that there's a slight difference in the LLC laws of each state.

   The operating agreement typically has a space that needs to be filled in for the registered agent. If your state's requirements allow it, you can be the one to fill in this space.

5. Check the "Business Purpose" section of your sample agreement and make sure it includes the statement that indicates your company's purpose as engaging in lawful acts or activities for which an LLC may be formed.

   You should also check the language in the "Term" section. "Indefinitely" is commonly used for the term.
   In the terms of dissolution, "by a majority" is also commonly used.

6. You should also check the language in the "Management" section.

   A majority of small shoe design businesses are managed by the members as a whole, but you also have the option of getting managers for your shoe design business, especially if there are active and passive members.

   Whatever you decide, make sure your agreement contains the appropriate language as to how your company will operate.

7. Personalize the sample agreement by inserting the data from the notes you took as per Step 1 and Step 2. Be sure to include the necessary signature lines.

8. Print the agreement as well as a list of all members with their respective addresses and then staple them together.

   Let all members sign the agreement, have it photocopied, and then provide each member with a copy.

   Be sure to keep the original somewhere safe and have additional copies in your files for reference.

Take note that this step-by-step guide does not constitute legal advice.

If there's anything about forming an LLC that you don't understand, it's still best to seek the advice of an attorney.

Writing a Company Brochure

A company brochure, also known as a corporate brochure, is an excellent way of introducing your shoe design business to your target market.

That is, of course, if you do it right.

The very first things you need to take into consideration are the logo, font, and color you use on your brochure.

People will only learn about your shoe design business if they read the brochure, and they are more likely to read a brochure if the cover has an attractive design, which is why your choice of logo, font, and color is very important.

Take note as well that people are more likely to patronize your shoe design business if you're able to build a connection with them and if you're able to establish in their minds the thought that you can be trusted.

The best way to do this using a brochure is to include pertinent information such as the background and history of your company, what you have to offer, and how you intend to deliver whatever it is you're offering. You may also include information on how your company intends to serve the community as a whole.

Furthermore, you'll need to provide an explanation of what the brochure itself is all about.

- Is it just about the organization or does it present the products and services as well?

- Is it all about the industry and what role your company plays in its development?

- Is it for a specific event where your company is a participant or is it a detailed brochure of your company?

And of course, you'll have to tell the reader at the outset what the brochure's relevance to him is.

Therefore, before you even start writing your company brochure, you'll first have to think about what you want the brochure to portray and who your target audience is.

You may want to set-up a brainstorming session with your company's key personnel for this purpose.
And take note that even as your brochure contains all the necessary information as discussed above, it should remain concise and easy to read.

You should also make it easy for the reader to select which particular piece of information he wants to read. This can be achieved through the use of headings and sub-titles.

As long as you keep these tips in mind, you should be able to create a company brochure that truly presents your shoe design business in a positive light.

With the brochures on hand, you may approach retail stores to see if they'd be interested in carrying your brand. Make sure your brochures contain an explanation of your brand's philosophy, the characteristics that make your shoes unique, and the benefits they gain by carrying your brand.

Leasing Space

Having enough space for your business not is one of the most critical factors in operating your new business as you don't need a shop or to hold any stock to speak of. However as your business grows you may need more space so I have included the basics of acquiring retail space here.

In choosing retail sales space, you'll have to take several things into consideration.

Among these things are good visibility of the location from the street, and easy access for your customers. You'll also have to decide if you're going to build, buy, or rent your retail sales space.

There are many advantages to renting space as opposed to buying or building.

Maintenance, flexibility, and taxes are perhaps the three most important advantages.

Maintenance

If you rent retail sales space, you'll be responsible only for a bit of routine maintenance issues like the replacement of light bulbs, repairing uninsured damages caused by negligence on your part, and cleaning the premises.

The good news for you is that major maintenance issues like electrical, plumbing, air conditioning, heating, and structural problems are the responsibility of your landlord.

This means that if your roof starts to leak, it will be your landlord's responsibility to have it repaired.

Knowing that your rent already covers major maintenance issues makes it so much easier for you to budget your company's available funds.

Flexibility

Renting space helps you avoid being forced to stay at the same location even when it's no longer practical to do so.

Even if you have a lease contract for a specific period, that's still a lot better than getting locked into a commercial mortgage.

If the demographics in your area change, then it will be much easier to relocate your shoe design business if you're simply leasing or renting space.

This also holds true for the time when your shoe design business has grown such that you need more space. Furthermore, you won't have to worry about selling your existing location if you have to move to a new place, which is an issue you'll have to deal with if you own the space.

Taxes

It's very easy to understand the advantages of renting space where taxes are concerned.

Rental payments are considered business expenses and are therefore deductible.

On the other hand, only the interest that you pay for commercial mortgages is deductible.

You have to consider as well, the fact that commercial property often doesn't appreciate as much as residential properties, which means your property may accrue very little equity over time.

When you weight this against the 100% deductibility of commercial rent, you'll realize how advantageous it is to simply lease retail space.

Now that you understand the benefits of leasing retail sales space, you'll have to learn how to find the perfect location for your shoe design business.

Remember that leasing will affect not only your company's profit, but also its ability to grow as well as the satisfaction level of your employees.

So, before you go out looking for space to rent, you'll have to know exactly what you are looking for. Here's how to identify the perfect retail sales space for your shoe design business:

1. Determine how much space your shoe design business needs now and how much it may need in the future. The rule of thumb in determining space requirements is to have 175-250 sq. ft. of space for each person who will be working at the location.

2. Contact a real estate agent and seek advice in finding a suitable commercial space.

   Agents typically have the inside scoop on what'd going on in the real estate market and they can advise you properly on which particular properties are ideal for your purposes.

It's a good idea to contact a real estate firm that specializes in office space rentals.

3. Discuss any necessary improvements with your potential landlord.

    Take note that improvements are usually subject to serious negotiations, especially if there are lots of vacancies.

    You would also do well to check out the parking space.

    Does the rental offer a number of slots you can set aside for yourself and your employees, or would you have to compete with the public for street parking?

4. You may be able to reduce rental cost by either sharing space or looking out for incubators.

    You could share your reception area, rest rooms, and conference rooms with another small firm to reduce your rental costs – that is, if you're okay with having less privacy.

    Incubators are small unused areas in a larger building which are usually offered for lease at much lower costs.

    These are also good options for a small shoe design business like yours, provided it meets with your requirements, of course.

5. You may also want to consider renting an all-inclusive suite.

   The rate for executive office suites is usually higher, but they usually come fully-furnished and provide you with access to meeting rooms and office equipment, thus significantly reducing your up-front costs.

   Many of these suites even come with a receptionist.

6. Before signing a lease contract, be sure to review it exhaustively.

   Check the indicated monthly payment, how long the lease is for, what maintenance and repair concerns the landlord will be responsible for, and things like annual rent increases in accordance with inflation.

   You'd also do well to check if there are provisions concerning the possibility of terminating the lease early as well as provisions regarding internet connections, cable service, telephone lines, and other company needs. Other important details for you to review include the date of occupancy, right of refusal for the adjoining space, security, and other amenities.

7. Finally, it's a good idea for you to hire a qualified real estate attorney.

   Make sure the attorney specializes in negotiations for leases and that he knows your area.

It's a bonus if he has dealt with the same kind of shoe design business in the past.

This is important because lease negotiations typically cover hundreds of terms, which makes it a definite advantage to have someone who's gone through it all before on your side.

Managing Your Employees

Once your shoe design business grows, you'll have to deal with managing your employees, which can be a very tricky process.

If you're not careful, you just might end up babysitting rather than running a successful shoe design business venture.

This is especially true if a majority of your employees are paid very low hourly rates.

You're lucky if you can hire wonderful employees who don't give you any problems.

However, you'll still have to find effective ways of keeping these wonderful employees in your shoe design business, and that's where good employee management comes in.

Perhaps the most important aspect of employee management is your ability to set very clear goals and communicate your company objectives very clearly to your employees.

Take note that goal-setting and communicating objectives have to be done regularly.

The more you communicate with your employees in an honest and open manner, the easier it will be for you to manage them. It's advisable to set monthly, quarterly, and annual goals. And you have to make sure the goals you set are mutual.

This means you should not be forcing your employees to work towards your own goals.

The employees themselves have to believe in those goals and they'll have to be taught how to adjust in case circumstances that keep them from attaining those goals suddenly arise.

Furthermore, you need to realize that goals don't really mean much unless employees' compensations are largely tied up with those goals.

The compensation may be in the form of bonuses, commissions, or salary percentages.

What's important is for the employees to have a good motivation for working towards the company's goals. It's also a good idea to hold a yearly meeting with all of your employees where an annual review will be conducted.

During this review, you should commend your employees for the things they're doing right and discuss solutions for the things that didn't quite work out. Identifying areas of improvement and finding solutions together can give employees the assurance that they really are part of the company and that they're being valued as individuals, not just as paid workers.

Finally, another very important part of employee management is getting feedback on how YOU are doing at your job.

- How are you as a manager?

- What are you doing right?

- What else can you do to become a better manager?

You have to realize that getting feedback from your employees isn't a waste of your time.

Quite the contrary, in fact.

More often than not, the best ideas for improving a shoe design business come from the front-liners, as they're usually the ones who know exactly what the customers want.

How to Market Your Shoe Design Business

Of course, you'll need to consider how you can get the word out about your new shoe design business.

After all, you can hardly succeed in any business venture unless people know of its existence, right?

Get to know the people involved in local fashion and start building your network. At the same time, you should also start building a reputation as a good shoe designer. Remember that marketing and promotion need to be an on-going effort. Participate in trade shows where you can showcase your designs. These events are excellent venues where you can widen your network and learn new marketing strategies and techniques.

You may also ask family and friends to show samples of your work to their social network. And speaking of networking, you can take advantage of the Internet by displaying samples of your work on your social network accounts. Word-of-mouth advertising, whether literal or the online version, is still the best way to spread the word about your shoe design business.

Always remember that the fashion industry is a competitive one and you'll need to remain updated on the latest styles and trends in order to succeed. You'll also need to try different approaches to promoting your work. Taking note of these things will bring you closer to success with your shoe design business.

Marketing your new shoe design business probably ranks among the most challenging aspects of putting up a business venture, not to mention that it can also be the most fun.

You should, in fact, be excited about marketing your shoe design business.

- The main purpose of marketing a shoe design business is to let your target customers know that you exist and that you have a lot of benefits to offer them.

And take note that the kind of message you convey to your target market is crucial when you market a new shoe design business.

Even if you're selling exactly the same item as your closest competitor, you're more likely to come out on top of the competition if you're able to come up with better marketing strategies and if you can successfully create a brand for your company.

Creating a brand for your company will make your shoe design business more valuable to potential customers. Regardless of what type of business you're into branding is still important.

In fact, the more you create an attractive personality around your company brand, the more you set yourself apart from the competition, thus giving your shoe design business a much better opportunity for growth.

How do you know your brand is effective?

Simple.

Market it to yourself.

Imagine that you're a would-be customer taking stock of a new player in the industry.

- Does the company brand look, sound, and feel authentic?

- Is it a fun and attractive brand?

Remember that marketing your shoe design business has to be fun, so don't take it too seriously.

And even while you're working hard to create a brand, you should always remain true to yourself.

That is what will make your brand truly authentic. And an authentic brand is something your competition can never take away.

In Conclusion...

By now you understand there are lots of things you need to take into serious consideration if you decide to establish your own shoe design business. Take note that these considerations go beyond choosing the right location for your business and setting a price schedule for your products.

Here's a quick overview:

Establishing partnerships

Unless you know how to create the shoes that you design, you'll definitely need someone to manufacture them for you. And if you don't have enough money saved up to cover start-up costs, then you'll need help financing the business as well. If this is the first time for you to ever set up a business venture, then you'd also do well to seek advice from an experienced entrepreneur.

Whatever the situation is, chances are good that you'll be needing help from someone else in establishing your shoe design business. Find a manufacturer who can transform your chosen designs from paper into actual shoes of good quality. It may be a good idea to look for a smaller manufacturer who'll be willing to make the shoes in small quantities initially until your shoe design business starts taking off and you can afford to get the shoes made in bulk.

Check out a few manufacturers and get quotations for the various designs as well as minimum order requirements and payment terms. Take some time to study the proposal of each manufacturer and then go with the one that can serve your needs best. Try to negotiate better terms as much as you can.

Cost

The cost of starting your own shoe design business depends largely on how much of the necessary equipment you already have. Basically, you need to have at least a computer, a reliable printer, and good design software. If you plan to establish a website for the business, then you'll need to factor the fees for site maintenance into the costs of the business.

Here's a tip:

Try to sell your shoes on eBay, Etsy or online flea markets. These options are relatively inexpensive and can tide you over until you can afford to set up your own website. Be sure to keep track of your finances using a notebook or reliable financing software.

Trends and sizes

Since you're establishing a design business, you'll have to check out the latest trends by visiting department stores and specialty boutiques, reading magazines, and attending fashion shows. You may also want to talk to family members, friends, and colleagues who belong to your target market about their preferences in shoes.

Protecting your designs

Making money out of your designs is indeed something to celebrate. However, you should guard yourself against getting too excited and forgetting to protect your work. Make sure you create a label for your shoe designs and then have the label copyrighted.

Take note that copyright processes differ from one country to the next, so you'll have to check the regulations that apply in your case.

And while you're checking into getting your work protected, you should also check out what paperwork you'll need to take care of for opening your shoe design business. Required permits and licenses also vary per country, so it's definitely a good idea to do some research.

Find a designer?

Many people think that in order to succeed in a shoe design business, they'll have to do the designing themselves.

That's not necessarily true. If you have good business skills and a natural love for shoes, but you don't really have the talent needed to create your own designs, you can still run a successful design business by hiring a good shoe designer. The designer can create entire collections, which you can launch on specific schedules within a year.

Each collection should have some common characteristics like the use of specific materials, an amazingly comfortable fit, or high-fashion look for affordable prices.

These common characteristics will become the key that makes your brand easily recognizable.

Price

Set a pricing schedule for your shoes. Make sure you've done your homework at this point and that the prices you set for your shoe line are appropriate for your target market while still turning up a good profit.

It's a good idea to set a retail price for individual customers and a trade price for other retail stores who may be interested in buying your shoes. Better yet, offer shoes in a wide range of prices so you can cater to a wider consumer base.

Association

Join a retailers or shoe manufacturers' association, as these organisations generally work to minimise trade restraints and regulate the industry.

By becoming an association member, you'll get the chance to keep up-to-date on valuable information and the latest news about the shoe design industry.

Get legal

Decide as to what legal structure your business will take and then register it accordingly.

Even if you're starting your shoe design business at home, you'll still need to get it registered so you won't have to deal with legal problems in the future.

Socialize

Use Facebook and Twitter to your advantageand raise
awareness about your brand. Take note that the more
people are made aware of your brand, the likelier you
will be to create a high demand for your shoes. Post
information on and photographs of your shoes on your
profile and then ask family and friends to share it on
their own profiles as well.

Keep going

Establishing your own shoe design business may be
rewarding, but nobody ever said it will be easy. You'll
have to prepare yourself for some hard work and be
armed with a great deal of patience and perseverance as
your business grows.

By keeping these tips in mind, you should be well on
your way towards attaining success with your very own
shoe design business.

Good luck!

6990496R00066

Made in the USA
San Bernardino, CA
20 December 2013